Golf's Funniest Anecdotes

about Arnie, Jack, Ben, Lee, Tiger, Sam, and All the Rest

Dick Crouser

 Meadowbrook Press

Distributed by Simon & Schuster
New York

Library of Congress Cataloging-in-Publication Data
Crouser, Dick.
    Golf's funniest anecdotes / by Dick Crouser.
        p.   cm.
    ISBN 0-88166-358-1 (Meadowbrook)—ISBN 0-743-21245-2
    (Simon & Schuster)
        1. Golf—Humor. 2. Golf—Anecdotes. I. Title.

GV967 .C74 2001
796.352—dc21   00-051140

Managing Editor: Christine Zuchora-Walske
Copyeditor: Joseph Gredler
Proofreader: Angela Wiechmann
Coordinating Editor: Megan McGinnis
Production Manager: Paul Woods
Desktop Publishing: Danielle White
Cover Art: George Karn
Illustrations: Jack Johnson

© 2001 by Dick Crouser

Published by Meadowbrook Press, 5451 Smetana Drive, Minnetonka, MN 55343

www.meadowbrookpress.com

BOOK TRADE DISTRIBUTION by Simon & Schuster, a division of Simon and Schuster, Inc., 1230 Avenue of the Americas, New York, NY 10020

05 04 03 02   10 9 8 7 6 5 4 3 2

Printed in the United States of America

Golf's Funniest Anecdotes

about Arnie, Jack, Ben, Lee, Tiger, Sam, and All the Rest

Dedication

For Dan, Mike, Jenny, and Pete,
four fine folks without whom
I wouldn't be a father.

Acknowledgments

We would like to thank the individuals who
served on reading panels for this project:

Phil Theibert, Leo Verrett, Jim Rallis, George Winsor,
Thomas Courage, Trevor Lloyd, Ned Pastor, Tim
Tocher, Dr. Paul Driscoll, Bob Zahn, Ron Tracy,
Norman Meltzer, John Foote, Gib Poiry, F. Blaine
Dickson, Frank Gredler, Marvin Wallace, Linda Cave,
Ron Zuchora-Walske, Dave Waldorf, Bruce Huffaker,
Patrick Bowyer

Introduction

When a fella can combine two of his favorite things and actually get paid for it, well, it just doesn't get any better than that. I'm kicked back in a lounge chair, surrounded by books and magazines, in search of the snappiest punch lines, the funniest put-downs, and the greatest comeback lines from the wonderful world of golf.

The missus, passing through and noticing that I seem to be enjoying myself rather excessively, interrupts, "What are you doing and why aren't you mowing the lawn?" "Sorry, dear," I reply solemnly, "I'm working."

Humor and golf. A delightful pair. A natural pair. Because with all its frustrations, tensions, absurdities, and cruel twists of fate, golf provides a rich and fertile field for humor.

Can any sport match it for fun and games? For fun and gamesmanship?

Well...baseball...maybe.

Baseball! Now, there's a thought.

Excuse me, won't you? I have work to do.

Working the British Open at Muirfield one year, broadcaster Ray Scott tried to make a quick visit to a nearby porta-potty. The line was long, but an elderly Scotsman standing ahead of Ray noticed him nervously checking his watch. With a gracious bow, the man said, "Would ye care to play through, laddie?"

Bantam Ben Hogan was called "The Iceman" both for his coolness under fire and for his aversion to small talk during a match. But Jimmy Demaret was quick to defend his old partner: "Hogan not very chatty? Nonsense," he said. "He'd speak to me on almost every green. He'd say, 'You're away.'"

Old-time comedian Jimmy Durante decided he'd like to try golf, so he took a couple of lessons and got a few buddies to join him on his first full round. It was a disaster. Jimmy barely broke 200. He wanted to do the right thing when the round ended, so he asked one of the guys what he should give the caddie. "Your clubs," the man answered.

How do Tiger Woods and Michael Jordan handicap each other when they go head-to-head in golf or basketball? According to Jordan, ten seems to be the operative number. Ten strokes for Jordan sounds about right, but should he give Tiger ten points at hoops? "I give him ten points and beat him in a game to eleven," explains Jordan, "and I give him the ball to start out."

Robert Trent Jones was never the pro golfer's favorite architect, because many pros felt that Jones had something against a golfer being able to shoot par. Jimmy Demaret, one of Jones's severest critics, ran into him once and said, "Saw a course you'd really like the other day, Trent. On the first tee, you take a penalty drop."

Bob Hope has played with many great golfers over the years and, presumably, has picked up a fair amount of free advice along the way. In return, he may have occasionally loaned his writers to some of the pros. Hope once asked Arnold Palmer to comment on his new swing, and Arnie replied, "I've seen better swings on a condemned playground."

Football official Jack Daly overheard a married couple he knows discussing what would happen if she died first. Wife: "I suppose you already have your eye on some pretty young thing to succeed me." Husband: "Maybe." Wife: "And I suppose you would have her share our bedroom." Husband: "Maybe." Wife: "And I suppose you would let her use my golf clubs." Husband: "Nope, she's left-handed."

Ken Venturi was having lunch at Winged Foot with member Jack Whitaker, and they decided to play a round. Since Venturi had neither clubs nor clothes, Whitaker borrowed some clubs and found him a tattered sweater and a ratty old hat. On the ninth fairway, Venturi was 2 under and had just hit a spectacular shot for an easy eagle putt. His caddie looked at him wide-eyed and said, "I don't know who you are, mister, but if you come back here tomorrow dressed like that, we can make a lotta money."

Los Angeles Times sportswriter Jim Murray was a slightly better writer than golfer. Okay, a lot better. He was once paired with pro Donna Caponi in an alternate-shot match, and he sorely tested her patience. She hit a booming tee shot; he scuffed one into the woods. She hit out of the woods onto the green; he putted off the green into the water. After several holes like this, she hit a big drive that stopped just in front of a water hazard. "What should I do here?" he asked. "Whiff it," she said.

What will those rascally Irish do next? A friend who returned recently from a golfing trip to Ireland reported seeing a notice posted outside the clubhouse of a course he played. It read, "Trousers are now allowed to be worn by ladies on the course, but they must be removed before entering the clubhouse."

A nasty part of the campaign against Dan Quayle when he was running for vice-president in 1988 was a bogus story put forth by a woman who claimed she had had a rendezvous with Quayle during a one-day golf trip he'd taken. It was quickly and confidently squelched by Marilyn Quayle, who said, "Anyone who knows Dan knows that given the choice between golf and sex, he'd take golf every time." The story died immediately.

E veryone knows J. C. Snead as, well, J. C. Snead. But a few years back, he revealed that his first name was Jesse and he'd like to be called that. A month later, he announced he'd like to be called J. C. again. Why? "Because Jesse isn't playing worth a damn," he said.

A rnold Palmer's slash-and-burn approach became his trademark early on and, until he mellowed a bit, got him into a lot of trouble. In one West Coast tournament, he had missed a green badly. As he was studying the unpleasant options, he noticed sports-writer Jim Murray in the gallery. "What would Hogan do in a spot like this, Jim?" he asked. "Hogan wouldn't be in a spot like that," said Murray.

One of golf's most difficult decisions is whether to try a shot from an awkward lie or to take a drop and the penalty that goes with it. Elaine Johnson's decision was easy. After she sliced a shot into a nearby tree, the ball bounced back and lodged in her halter top. "I'll take the penalty," she said. "I absolutely refuse to play it where it lies."

Before there was John Daly and Tiger Woods, there was Jim Dent, a guy who could crush the ball off the tee. However, big hitters tend to be a bit erratic now and then. As Dent put it, "Sure I can airmail the ball, but sometimes I have the wrong address on it."

Most average golfers' swing problems will seem pretty minor if they have a chance to watch a tournament of blind players. There they'll see true resolve and dedication—and a bit of humor, too. Once, blind golfer Charlie Boswell was standing near a tee box while an opponent was hitting. After the swing, Boswell shook his head and muttered, "Worst swing I've ever heard!"

Bob Hope was playing a round with film mogul Sam Goldwyn when Sam missed a short putt and, in a rage, threw the putter away. On the way to the next hole, Hope picked up the offending putter and put it in his bag while Goldwyn wasn't looking. Two holes later, Hope used the reclaimed putter to drain a long one. "Great shot," said Goldwyn. "Let me see that club." He looked it over and said, "I like this putter. I'll give you fifty bucks for it." "Done," said Hope.

Once, near the end of one of his high-volume, temperamental, club-throwing rounds, Tommy Bolt asked his caddie to recommend a club for a 155-yard shot. "I'd say either a 3-iron or a wedge, sir," said the caddie. "A 3-iron or a wedge?" said Bolt. "What kind of stupid choice is that?" "Those are the only clubs you have left, sir," said the caddie.

During the 1991 Ryder Cup matches, Paul Azinger caused a big flap by calling NBC analyst Johnny Miller "the biggest moron I've ever seen in the booth." As the controversy grew, Azinger protested that he had been misquoted. What did he claim to have said? "I called him the biggest *Mormon* I'd ever seen in the booth."

Talk about the power of suggestion. John F. Kennedy was playing a round at Seminole with its chairman, Chris Dunphy. On the first green, Kennedy faced a 3-footer and said, "Is this good, Chris?" Dunphy replied, "Oh, I don't know, why don't you putt that one." Kennedy responded, "Oh, by the way, I can't dawdle. I have a meeting with the head of the IRS in a few hours." Dunphy replied, "The putt's good, Jack."

Jackie Burke was a successful pro golfer back in the thirties, but he never had much luck against the immortal Byron Nelson. Burke was especially frustrated by Nelson's consistency off the tee. "The only time Byron Nelson ever left the fairway," said Burke, "was to go pee in the woods."

B abe Didrikson Zaharias is considered by many to be the best female athlete of all time. She set world records at the Olympics, starred in softball, and won seventeen tournaments in a row on the women's pro golf tour. Writer Paul Gallico once asked Babe if there were any game she didn't play as a kid. "Yes," she said, "dolls I didn't play."

A t last, the answer to a duffer's problems: Buy your own golf course. When asked what par was for the course he had just bought, singer Willie Nelson said, "Anything I want it to be. This hole right here, for example, is a par-47," said Nelson, "and yesterday I birdied the sucker."

J immy Demaret was known to indulge in a cocktail now and then. So it came as no surprise to the other members of his Pro-Am foursome when he showed up one day at the first tee with a Big-Bertha-size hangover. Asked if he had ever considered giving up the stuff, Jimmy replied, "Not a chance. That would mean waking up in the morning knowing that that's as good as I'm going to feel all day."

The caddies at St. Andrew's know their business and are not reluctant to speak their minds. Finishing up a terrible round there, two Americans had just teed off on the 18th. They were walking across the stone bridge that spans the Swilcan Burn when one of them looked down gloomily and declared, "If that water were deep enough, I'd throw my clubs in and then drown myself." "Not possible, sir," his caddie said. "You couldn't keep your head down long enough."

One of the interests Jack Nicklaus developed after conquering golf was wine. Nicklaus and writer Dick Taylor were once seated together at a PGA dinner, when Taylor decided to test Nicklaus's knowledge of the subject. As several bottles of fine wine wrapped in linen were delivered to their table, Taylor challenged Nicklaus to identify each one sight unseen. Nicklaus swirled and tasted—and identified each precisely. Later, Taylor mentioned to Deane Beman how impressed he had been with Nicklaus's skills. "He should have known them all," said Beman. "He's the one who picked them for the dinner."

TV analyst David Feherty remembers some medical advice that didn't work for his golfing father, William, back in Ireland's County Down. A physician tried to cure the elder Feherty's insomnia by encouraging him to play an imaginary round of golf in his head while lying in bed. Reporting back to the doctor, William said, "I played great until the third tee shot, which I sliced into the woods. Then I was awake all night looking for the ball."

Before a banquet at which former Notre Dame football coach Ara Parseghian was to speak, the master of ceremonies wanted to make sure he would pronounce Parseghian's name correctly. So he took the coach aside and asked him for a pronunciation tip. "Just remember it this way," said Ara. *"Par* as in golf, *segh* as in Seagrams, and *yan* as in Chinese." When the time came, the MC announced, "I can't remember his name, but here is that famous drunken Chinese golfer."

As Sam Snead grew older, he gave fewer and fewer lessons and became increasingly impatient with his pupils. After a particularly frustrating session with one inept fellow, Sam's final advice was, "I think you should lay off for about three weeks and then give up the game altogether."

After Mike Mazzeo had caddied for Fuzzy Zoeller for more than fifteen years, he was asked to reveal the secret of his longevity in an occupation noted for its rapid turnover. Was it his club-selection skills, his knowledge of courses, his rock-steady demeanor under pressure? "No," said Mazzeo. "After twenty years, I know too much. He's afraid to fire me."

In his prime, Arnold Palmer's positive, go-for-it style endeared him to a whole generation of golf fans. He dripped with confidence. Gene Littler was especially impressed with Palmer's attitude on the greens. "I'm always surprised when one of my putts drops," Littler said, "but it never occurs to Arnold that his ball won't go in the hole."

Sandy Lyle takes issue with the old saying, "It's not whether you win or lose, it's how you play the game." "No, no, the emphasis is all wrong there," Lyle says. "It's not whether *you* win or lose, it's whether *I* win or lose."

Nick Faldo had just won the biggest purse of his life—a cool $1 million—and was feeling generous when he asked his wife if there were anything she'd like to have. "A divorce," she said. "I wasn't thinking of anything quite that expensive," Faldo replied.

Basketball great Bill Russell wasn't always the avid golfer he became once his remarkable career with the Celtics ended. "When I was growing up, my mother wouldn't let me near a golf course," said Russell. "She didn't think golfers were very nice people. And now that I play every day, I realize she was right."

Claude Harmon's son Dick never matched his dad's exploits on the tour, but Dick became a great teacher of the game. Lanny Wadkins once came to Houston for a session with Dick at a time when Claude was also in town, and the three of them played a round. At one point, Lanny hit a tremendous downhill-lie 3-wood about 2 feet from the pin on a guarded green. "Tell me, son," Claude said to Dick, "what is it you plan to teach this young man?"

Rank does have its privileges. President Dwight Eisenhower had a few odd habits on the golf course that no one ever challenged. For example, he used a club to roll his ball over on the fairway on the pretext of identifying it. Coincidentally, this action often resulted in a better lie. When he once tried to roll it over in the rough, his ball became lodged against a rock. "What happened?" Ike asked his caddie. "I'm afraid you've over-identified your ball, Mr. President," the caddie responded.

The high cost of living (or playing) is bothering pro athletes, too. With everything from golf balls to bowling balls shooting up in price, former bowling great Don Carter still thinks he chose the right sport. "You seldom lose a bowling ball," said Carter.

Doesn't it get boring for the pro golfer to play every hole in regulation? Drive down the middle, hit the green, and then two-putt. Why not take a few chances and have some fun? Lee Trevino tells us why not: "There are two things that are not long for this world," he says. "Dogs who chase cars and golfers who chip for pars."

What's so tough about Pennsylvania's Oakmont Country Club course? Well, the greens, for one thing. Some say that putting there is like trying to stop a ball halfway down a flight of marble steps. Sam Snead claimed that he once marked a ball on an Oakmont green and the marker slid downhill.

The legendary Walter Hagen was as famous for his late-night barroom adventures as he was for his exploits on the golf course. And no one ever accused him of being short on self-confidence. On one occasion, it was past midnight on the eve of a big match, and a concerned bartender tried to convince Hagen to get some shuteye. "Your opponent's been in bed for hours," the bartender said. "Young man," said Hagen, "he may have retired, but he knows whom he's playing tomorrow, and you may be sure he hasn't slept a wink."

Forget about all the tournaments Tommy Bolt has won and all the money he's taken home; his name will forever be associated with club throwing. And as the ultimate authority on the subject, he frequently dispenses advice. For example, "Always throw the club forward so you can pick it up on your way down the fairway." Jimmy Demaret once described Bolt's credentials on the subject: "Tommy Bolt's putter has had more air time than Lindbergh."

Jack Nicklaus's skills and his performances over the years are the stuff of legends. But it would seem he hasn't received enough credit for his teaching ability and his tips for playing the game. When explaining why one should tee the ball high, for example, Nicklaus says, "Years of experience have shown me that air offers less resistance than dirt."

Show biz people have traditionally loved the game of golf. Bob Hope, Jack Lemmon, Dean Martin, to name just a few. And they've enjoyed hanging around the big hitters at tournaments. But many Hollywood stars have been sensitive about revealing their scores. Old-time comedian Joe E. Lewis neatly avoided the subject when he said, "I usually play in the low 80s. If it's any warmer than that, I don't go out."

Craig Stadler doesn't throw his clubs as often or as far as Tommy Bolt, but his style is good and his range is pretty decent. Once, after watching Stadler hole out on 18, a friend asked him why he was using a new putter. "Because my old one didn't float," Stadler replied.

Lee Trevino has been hit by lightning on the golf course and has not enjoyed the experience. So he's settled on a policy of rapidly fleeing the course when it starts to rain or lightning. "When God wants to play through, I let him play through," he says.

Back in the days when tournament purses were a bit more modest than they are today, Ben Hogan demonstrated his practical side. He initiated the custom of the Masters winner hosting the following year's Champions Dinner. But after winning one year, Hogan seemed to have a change of heart. "When I discovered that the cost of the dinner was more than the prize money," he said, "I finished second four times."

My friend Kent once described the day he quit playing golf: "I'm playing with a couple of strangers. Playing lousy. Hooks, slices, shanks. Depressing. We come to a par-3 elevated tee where you shoot over a deep, dark pond. I scuff my 7-iron into the damn pond. I pop another one into the damn pond. I dribble a third one into the damn pond. I lose control and throw the damn 7-iron out into the pond. I grab the damn bag and throw it into the pond. I turn around and these two guys are staring at me bug-eyed. The one guy says, 'I can't believe you did that.' The other guy says, 'I can't believe you did that either. That was my bag!'"

It was the third round of the Los Angeles Open, and Arnold Palmer needed only a par on 18 to give him a 69 and the lead. But he hit his second shot out-of-bounds. Then he hit another OB. And another. He finally limped in with a horrendous 12. "How in the world could you make a 12?" a reporter asked Arnie. "I missed a 20-footer for my 11," said Palmer.

Ben Crenshaw was eight years old the first time he came to Harvey Penick for a lesson. Harvey cut down a 7-iron and asked Ben to hit a ball to a green about 75 yards away. He did. "Good," said Harvey, "now take this putter and go up and putt the ball into the hole." "Why didn't you tell me to do that on the first shot?" asked Ben.

They grow their golfers tough in Canada. When C. Arthur Thompson was in his nineties, he often shot his age or better. When he reached 105, C. A. got a nice surprise from those big spenders at the Upland Golf Club in Victoria: A life membership!

Many pro golfers are associated with their individual characteristics. Lee Trevino is glib, Arnold Palmer is flamboyant, Ben Hogan was tight-lipped. How about Tom Lehman? Well, according to Justin Leonard, the word for Tom is "straight arrow." After playing a round with Lehman, Leonard said, "We didn't speak for fifteen holes because I couldn't think of a clean joke to tell him."

Despite their numerous heroics, athletes are sometimes remembered for the one glaring mistake they made. Bill Buckner for the World Series grounder that went through his legs. Chris Webber for the ill-fated time-out in the NCAA finals. Doug Sanders for the 2-foot putt that would have won him the British Open in 1970. Does Sanders still think about that putt after all these years? "Oh, I sometimes go as long as four or five minutes without thinking about it," he says.

If eccentric Scandinavian golfer Jesper Parnevik thinks of himself as a fashion setter, he should think again. His bill-turned-up baseball cap trademark has never quite caught on here in America. When describing Jesper's peculiar style, sportswriter Dan Jenkins said, "Parnevik always looks like the last guy to climb out of the clown car at the circus."

The 1999 NEC Invitational at Firestone's tough South Course featured many American and European players already selected for the upcoming Ryder Cup matches. After ballooning to an 80 in Friday's round, José Maria Olazabal was reminded that he still holds the course record: a fabulous 61 in 1990. "I remember that day's round very well," said Olazabal. "I just can't recall how I did it."

Los Angeles Times writer and frustrated golfer Jim Murray was optimistic about the afterlife. "I'm betting that when St. Peter discovers I was a golfer, he'll step aside and say, 'Go right in. You've suffered enough.'"

Most golfers have two handicaps: the numerical one and the physical one. For comedian Jackie Gleason, the physical one was quite obviously his waistline. "When I put the ball where I can see it, I can't hit it," he said. "And when I put it where I can hit it, I can't see it."

Things were a lot simpler back in the forties and fifties when the big golf tournaments were not very big at all. But with growth comes red tape and the loss of spontaneity. When the idea of having players wear numbers on their backs was introduced at one of the majors, some golfers didn't like it. But Jimmy Demaret said, "For the kind of money they're paying here, I'd wear a skirt."

P. G. Wodehouse wrote dozens of stories about golf that had great insight into the foibles and frustrations of golfers. In the happy ending to one of his tales, the hero says, "He enjoys that perfect peace, that peace beyond all understanding, which comes at its maximum only to the man who has given up golf."

Cary Middlecoff, the "golfing dentist" and one of the top players of the forties and fifties, was noted for his annoyingly slow play. Writer Dan Jenkins claims that Middlecoff finally gave up dentistry because none of his patients could hold their mouths open that long.

When John Daly first appeared on the tour, those in the golfing world tried to find ways to describe his booming drives. Gay Brewer said, "I can't even point that far." Fuzzy Zoeller chipped in, "By the time we walk up to his drive, my clothes have gone out of style." And writer Bob Verdi said, "He's longer than Couples or Norman. He's longer than Tolstoy!"

During one Pro-Am, Chi Chi Rodriguez was waiting patiently at greenside while an inept partner made four or five futile attempts to escape a bunker. Finally, after another unsuccessful blast, Chi Chi said, "If you dig any deeper, you might find Jimmy Hoffa!"

Sam Snead was playing a practice round at Augusta National with the much younger Bobby Cole (with a few bucks riding on the match, of course). Reaching the tee at the dogleg-left par-5, Snead said, "You know Bobby, when I was your age, I'd drive the ball right over those trees at the corner." Feeling challenged, Bobby hit a big drive right *into* the big trees. Snead said, "Of course, when I was your age, those trees were only ten feet high."

When Jack Stephens took over as chair of the Augusta National Golf Club, he was a very wealthy man. Yet he never flaunted his money. He was offended, therefore, by a guest who made a great show of his wealth. As the two were preparing to play a round, Stephens suggested a two-dollar nassau. The man scoffed that he never played for less than a hundred dollars. Later, as they sat down to play gin, Stephens suggested they play for a penny a point. When the man insisted on a dollar a point, Stephens had had enough. "How much are you worth, sir?" he asked. "Twelve million," said the man. "Shall we cut the cards for your twelve million?" said Stephens. He was serious.

Japanese golfer Tommy Nakajima, whose golf was better than his English, was doing well in the first round of the Masters a few years ago, until the par-5 13th. At the end of that disaster, he had used 13 strokes. Later, he was asked if he had lost his composure on that hole. "No lose composure," he said. "Lose count."

Dicky Pride struck a blow for the anti–cell phone movement at the 1999 Honda Classic at Coral Springs, Florida. While lining up a putt, his concentration was broken by a spectator's phone ringing just beyond the gallery ropes. Pride said, "Excuse me, sir, I'm working here. If you have to work, would you please go to your office."

Chi Chi Rodriguez's first love is, of course, golf. It's not that he hasn't tried other sports. He's just found them wanting. Take tennis, for example. "Getting two serves is unfair," says Chi Chi. "The guy can wind up and blast one at you, and if he misses, he gets a mulligan."

Playing in the 1964 Crosby Clambake, Arnold Palmer had a problem. Coming up the 17th fairway, he had hit a shot down the cliff and into the Pacific Ocean. Someone asked TV commentator Jimmy Demaret what choices Palmer had for his next shot. "I don't know," said Demaret. "His nearest drop from there would be Honolulu."

The thrill and drama of the last-round comeback has made tournament golf a huge spectator draw. Palmer, Nicklaus, Woods, Love, Faldo—they've all done it. Roger Maltbie has, too, although he didn't seem to possess the supreme confidence golf miracles normally require. Ten strokes back entering the last round of an Andy Williams tourney, he was asked what he'd have to shoot to win. "The rest of the field," he said.

As a substantial number of wounded spectators can verify, some of our twentieth-century presidents have reputations for hitting the golf ball a bit erratically. At a recent Bob Hope Classic, as a member of the group that included Gerald Ford, George Bush, and Bill Clinton was getting ready to hit from the first tee, Barbara Bush was heard to say, "As if we don't have enough violence on television."

In the no-holds-barred-as-long-as-you're-not-caught world of hustler golf, here's a beauty. A high-stakes game was tied as darkness fell and the twosome finished putting on the par-3 18th. As they discussed replaying 18 for all the marbles, "Joe" took his opponent's ball from the hole and flipped it to him, but covertly left his own ball in the cup. Back on the tee, in almost total darkness, Joe belted one well beyond the flag while hollering, "Yes! In the hole! Get in the hole!" They arrived at the green to find that (surprise) Joe had a hole-in-one.

Tommy Bolt was in an ugly mood one day, and on the first tee he told his caddie he didn't want to hear a single word from him. Late in the round, Bolt found himself with a difficult shot and asked the caddie what he thought about a 5-iron. Following Bolt's instructions, the caddie said nothing. Bolt proceeded to hit a great shot and said, "Well, what the hell do you think of that?" Breaking his silence at last, the caddie said, "That wasn't your ball, Mr. Bolt."

Ben Crenshaw, like most golf pros, has had his share of highs and lows over the years. The highs have been spectacular, and the lows have been, well, let him explain: "I went fishing a couple of weeks ago," he says, "and on my first cast I missed the lake."

Near the end of Gene Littler's career, his dwindling game resulted in fewer purses and smaller galleries. Following one round, however, he came into the players' lounge with a huge smile and said, "Well, I guess I've still got the old charisma. Had a huge gallery out there today." Someone asked who his partner was. "Palmer," he said offhandedly.

Ben Crenshaw has kept improving through the years, but his biggest problem has been periodic lapses in concentration. At one point during one of his more successful periods, a reporter asked him how far he thought he was from being ranked among the best. "About five inches," said Ben. "The distance between my ears."

It ain't who you know, it's what you've done. Or perhaps what you've won. Lee Trevino claims that when he first came on the tour, he smiled and laughed and told jokes, and no one paid any attention to him. "Then, in 1968, I won the U.S. Open," he says. "I told the same jokes, did the same routines, and everybody laughed like hell."

The player with the most glamorous nickname in the fifties and sixties was Champagne Tony Lema. In private, he probably didn't imbibe enough of the bubbly to warrant the name, but he still enjoyed the notoriety. Once, when asked by a reporter to reveal how much he drank, Tony said, "Not as much as you do." "How do you know that?" asked the man. "Because only a drunk would ask the question," said Lema.

Charles Blair McDonald, the designer of Long Island's National Golf Links of America, was a rich and powerful man. And he strongly resented even the slightest criticism of his golf course. When his nephew, Peter Grace, announced that the 320-yard first hole was so short that he himself could drive it, McDonald demanded that he prove it. They strode to the first tee and Grace put a drive right up next to the pin. Without saying a word, McDonald walked into the clubhouse, called his lawyer, and wrote Grace out of his will.

One year, Billy Joe Patton was on the second hole of a sudden-death playoff in the North and South Amateur at Pinehurst. His opponent was on in two, but Billy Joe's second shot was buried under the lip of a fairway bunker. As he struggled for some footing for an impossible shot, a car stopped on the greenside road and a man yelled, "Anybody know where I can get a room?" "If you wait a couple of minutes," said Billy Joe, "you can probably have mine."

Ken Venturi's life was at its lowest ebb in 1964. His game, his marriage, and his finances were all in shambles, and he was ready to quit the tour. Then, in one of professional sports' most dramatic comebacks, he won the U.S. Open and his career flourished again. By 1974, he was playing only part-time and was out of contention at the U.S. Open at Winged Foot. Struggling up one of the final fairways, he heard a man in the gallery say, "If I were him, I'd quit." Venturi was cheered to hear the man's companion say, "Yeah, and if you were him you'd have quit ten years ago, too."

Ben Hogan was never much for giving free advice. He once had a playing partner who complained constantly about his putting, especially his long approach putts. Finally, the man asked Hogan if he had any tips. "Did you ever think about hitting them closer to the hole?" Ben said.

Dutch Harrison's partner in one Pro-Am got to be a bit aggravating. He'd press Dutch for advice on almost every shot, and then botch it. Late in the round, he found his drive under a thick evergreen and said, "How shall I play it, Dutch?" "Under an assumed name," said Harrison.

We know that Jimmy Demaret was a fine golfer. A great golfer. So we can probably assume he didn't have himself in mind when he said, "Golf and sex are the only things you can enjoy without being good at them."

Like a number of staid old clubs, the Royal St. George's at Sandwich, England, banned women from the course for many years. This policy became a problem when the Cambridge University team came to Royal St. George's for their annual match, and it was discovered that Miss Fiona MacDonald was on the Cambridge roster. Proving once again why "there'll always be an England," the Royal St. George's committee sat down over brandy and cigars and hammered out a solution: They declared MacDonald an honorary man.

The curse of the public golf course is slow play—the six-hour round. But even a few pros suffer from slow-play disease. Like Bernhard Langer, according to some. He and Lee Trevino were paired for a round in 1992, and as Trevino was coming off the 18th green, he was asked to comment on Langer's new beard: "He was clean-shaven when we teed off."

Walter Hagen knew his approach shot had landed in a greenside bunker, but until he got there, he didn't realize it had rolled into a paper bag. He asked an official for a ruling and was told he'd either have to play it from inside the bag or take a drop and a penalty stroke. Walter had other ideas. He lit a cigarette, dropped the match onto the bag, and watched as the bag burned away. He then proceeded to get up and down for his par.

Playing in a tournament on an Arizona desert course, Gary Player became upset after hearing that three snakes had been killed during that day's round. He explained that snakes wouldn't bother people if they were left alone. Dave Stockton's answer was, "They won't bother you if they're dead, either."

Americans playing a round in Scotland are often impressed with how seriously the game is taken there. One Yank learned the lesson very quickly at a Scottish course. His very first drive hooked out-of-bounds, so he teed up another ball and hit it right down the middle. Turning to the caddie he said, "In America we call that a mulligan. What do you call it here?" "We call it lying three," said the caddie.

After a chiropractor adjusted the backbones of an avid but high-handicap golfer, the patient said with relief, "It's starting to feel better, Doc. Tell me, do you think this'll improve my game?" The chiropractor answered, "Joe, I can heal the sick, but I can't raise the dead."

In the 1990 PGA Seniors tournament, Jack Nicklaus found himself with a very difficult bunker shot. After a couple of unsuccessful attempts to extricate himself, Jack was fuming. "Who designed this #*+! bunker?" he moaned. His rage turned to sheepishness, however, when an official pointed out that he, Nicklaus, had designed the course.

If you walk into a tournament and see a hulking giant whaling away at the golf ball, you have to figure it's a Pro-Am and the guy is a football player. Because, with the exception of John Daly, you don't see many really big guys at golf's top level. But in 1990, the 300-pound-plus Chris Patton won the U.S. Amateur and was in the headlines for a while. Tiny Gary Player was impressed. "Patton is the only player I know," he said, "who takes a divot just standing there."

Playing mixed doubles tennis with your spouse is a bad idea. And, according to Bryan Tenneson, the same goes for making your spouse your caddie. Playing in the second round of the 1987 U.S. Open, Tenneson was struggling to make the cut when he blew a simple 3-foot par putt. Looking to his wife/caddie for solace, he heard her growl, "You choked!" His response? "I fired her on the spot," said Tenneson.

How has the U.S. income tax system made golfers a little more respectable? Will Rogers had the answer: "The income tax has made liars out of more Americans than golf has."

Before David Feherty became a TV analyst, he was a moderately successful touring pro. But in 1995, his game and his marriage fell apart at about the same time. Before finally getting straightened out, he dealt with his problems in two ways, both a bit extreme. He went on what he calls his divorce diet (coffee, cigarettes, Advil, and alcohol), and he started running a hundred miles a week. The net result? "I lost 40 pounds," he says. "150 if you include my wife."

Chi Chi Rodriguez did okay on the regular PGA Tour, but not nearly as well as he's done on the over-fifty Senior Tour. In fact, he's looking forward to keeping the good times rolling by creating a Really Old Guys Tour (over eighty). "You'll play three-day tournaments, shooting one hole each day," he says. "Then the guy who can remember each of his three scores wins the money."

Tom Lehman has learned that every round of golf teaches you something, even in a mixed, alternate-shot tournament. At the first hole, Tom hit his tee shot about 275 yards. His wife, Melissa, shanked the ball into the rough. Tom then hit out of the rough to within 10 feet of the pin, only to have Melissa send her putt 25 feet past the cup. After Tom sank the comebacker, he suggested to her that she'd have to do a little better if they were to contend. She responded, "Hey, you took three shots. I took only two!"

When Gary McCord was playing on the PGA Tour, he criticized courses and conditions quite vocally. And that behavior didn't stop when he became a TV analyst and a player on the Senior Tour. One year, playing with the seniors at the Greater Greensboro Open, he was especially unhappy about the water-lined 13th. After watching one drive hook into the water on the left and another get wet on the right, he snapped, "They should just flood the fairway and make the whole thing a lake."

Back in 1990, a writer realized that, dating all the way back to 1927, only three foreign golfers had won the U.S. Open. He asked Seve Ballesteros if he had a theory about why this was so. "It's no big deal," said Seve. "How many Americans have won the Spanish Open?"

Not wanting to miss the pre-tournament dinner, Mark Calcavecchia arrived early at the 1990 British Open. When he learned that fifteen former champions were in attendance, he wanted all of their autographs. He was dismayed, however, when he collected only fourteen signatures. Greg Norman finally pointed out that *he,* Calcavecchia, was the fifteenth winner.

In 1990, before the floodgates opened on big commercial sponsorships of golf tournaments, Bruce Meadows, a reporter for the *Santa Rosa Press Democrat,* was not happy that the Greater Greensboro Open had become the K-Mart Greater Greensboro Open. Rumor has it Meadows once reported that the $150,000 purse for first place had been marked down to $129,050.

Sam Snead and his manager, Fred Corcoran, were touring Europe one year. When they arrived in Rome, Corcoran arranged an audience with the Pope and encouraged Snead to bring his putter so the Pontiff could bless it. The monsignor who met them at the Vatican revealed that he was also a golfer and was having serious problems with his putting. As Snead put away his putter, he told the monsignor, "If you're a buddy of the Pope and you can't putt, he ain't gonna do anything for me."

Lee Trevino does things the old-fashioned way: He keeps it simple. No personal trainer, no public relations specialist, no traveling nutritionist—just Trevino and his caddie. When asked if he would ever consider consulting a swing coach, Trevino said, "When I find one who can beat me, I'll listen."

To Jimmy Demaret's well-known talents as a golfer and TV analyst, add his abilities with a crystal ball. During the 1958 Masters, Arnold Palmer had hit his tee shot to the very back of the tricky par-3 16th green. "There's no way he gets down in two from back there," predicted Demaret. Palmer proceeded to chip the ball into the hole for a birdie. "See?" said Demaret.

There were mixed feelings about the merits of the Traveling Fitness Center when it first showed up on the PGA Tour in 1987. Gay Brewer noted, however, that it was getting a fair amount of attention. "Even Billy Casper is in there pedaling away on the bike," he said. "Of course, he rode a golf cart to get over there."

What impressed some people about Ben Hogan was his total concentration during a match. Nothing could distract him. For example, at a Masters in the early fifties, Hogan was paired with Claude Harmon. Hogan hit first at the par-3 12th and put his shot about 10 feet from the pin. Harmon did better, putting his tee shot into the hole for an ace, and the crowd went wild. After calmly sinking his birdie putt, Hogan said, "You know, Claude, I've been waiting a long time to make a 2 on that hole."

South African golfer Simon Hobday is normally an easygoing fellow who steers clear of controversy. When he does run afoul of the rules, he chooses his words carefully. He once asked an official, "If I called you an S.O.B., would you fine me?" "Probably," said the official. "How about if I were just *thinking* it?" Hobday said. "No. How could I?" replied the official. "Okay, then, I *think* you're an S.O.B.," said Hobday.

Even the immortal Bobby Jones had his off days, so Miller Barber didn't panic when he found himself in an extended slump. He couldn't seem to put anything on the fairway. "The way I'm playing right now," Barber said, "if I took up gardening and grew tomatoes, they'd come up sliced."

The incredible success with which Tiger Woods began his professional career prompted Brad Faxon to suggest that a notation be added to the record books. "If you win a tournament and Tiger didn't play in it," said Faxon, "there should be an asterisk next to your name."

Professional athletes travel a lot, and married ones need spouses who are considerate, sympathetic, and understanding. "My wife doesn't care what I do when I'm away," says Lee Trevino, "as long as I don't have a good time."

Donald Ross was a Scot who came to America and became one of the best golf architects of all time. He was immensely proud of his work and was not above promoting his courses. In a telegram to the winner of a tournament at one of his courses, he wrote, "Excellent, the greatest!" The man wired back, "Not deserving of such praise." Ross responded, "Was referring to the course." The man replied, "So was I."

During his two terms in the White House, Dwight Eisenhower did a lot to popularize golf. However, politics being the unsavory business it is, his detractors turned his love for the game against him during the 1956 election. They circulated a poster that read, "Ben Hogan for president. If we're going to have a golfer, let's have a good one."

Alex Karras has a way with words. During his football career with the Detroit Lions, he was asked about charges that he had overstayed his eligibility at Iowa. He responded, "I was at Iowa for just two terms—Truman's and Eisenhower's." Later, he was equally candid on the golf course. Playing at Michigan's Red Run Golf Club, he sliced his first drive through the large window in the clubhouse dining room. Trudging over, he peered through the shattered glass and asked, "Is this room out-of-bounds?"

The new Ocean Trails course in Rancho Palos Verdes suffered a bit of a setback in June of 1999 when the 18th hole slid down a bluff toward the Pacific Ocean. Writer Jerry Perisho tried to look on the bright side. "Sure, the 18th fairway now has a twenty-six-thousand acre sand trap and a water hazard that stretches all the way to Japan," he said, "but now everyone gets to hit from the ladies' tee."

Jimmy Demaret and Ben Hogan were long-time rivals, but they admired each other greatly. Demaret was standing in a bar one night when someone told him that Hogan once said that if Jimmy were to practice more and party less, he'd win every tournament he entered. Demaret, pleased with the observation, lifted his glass and said, "I'll drink to that!"

Chi Chi Rodriguez has amassed a pretty impressive record of tournament wins. But he marvels at the incredible string of majors and other victories Jack Nicklaus has rung up. Even with his reduced schedule, Nicklaus is formidable, Chi Chi says. "Today," he adds, "he's a legend in his spare time."

Ben Hogan's well-known insistence on privacy extended to his work with the few pupils he took on. A writer once asked Kris Tschetter if she could discuss what Ben had helped her with. "I could tell you, of course," she said, "but then I'd have to kill you."

Pittsburgh sportswriter Bob Drum wanted his newspaper to send him to the British Open to cover the exploits of a hot young golfer named Arnold Palmer. His editor refused, but Drum went anyway at his own expense. To everyone's surprise, Palmer was in contention going into the final round. Drum received a wire from his editor that read, "Need a thousand words on Palmer." Drum wired back, "Hope you get it."

Lyndon Johnson was one of the few twentieth-century U.S. presidents who could not be accused of being a golfer. He showed up as a spectator at the Masters one year, but his motives were political. Not aware of Johnson's indifference to the game, someone at Augusta asked him what his handicap was. "Congress," said Johnson.

Bob Trumpy was a very good football player. When he retired and became a sports announcer, some people thought he was pretty good at that, too. But they didn't think his announcing skills extended to golf. After hearing Trumpy handle some Ryder Cup matches, the *San Francisco Chronicle*'s Mark Solatu delivered this critique: "Bob Trumpy doesn't know a graphite shaft from an elevator shaft."

Jack Nicklaus got off to a somewhat shaky start in the 1991 Tradition. After the first two rounds, he found himself 12 strokes behind the leader. But then he regained his edge and fired rounds of 66 and 67 to win the tournament and the sizeable first-place check. Afterward, someone asked Frank Beard if he thought Nicklaus was really that good. "No," Beard replied, "he's been on a thirty-year lucky streak."

John Daly has had a lot of problems during his career, but no one can doubt his fierce determination to win or his sense of style. He has said publicly that he would do almost anything to win a tournament. Why *almost?* "Well, I'm sure as hell not going to wear knickers," he explained.

We're indebted to one of Tommy Bolt's regular partners for this tale, although he prefers to remain anonymous. Tommy had just blown an iron shot and, in a rage, threw the offending club into the nearby lake. "You'd better throw a provisional," said our contributor. "That one's probably lost."

Two masters of their respective sports, Ted Williams and Sam Snead, were discussing the relative difficulties of their games. Williams maintained that nothing could be harder than hitting a baseball coming at you at a hundred miles an hour. "Maybe so," said Snead, "but you don't have to go into the stands and play your foul balls like we do."

When a player and caddie are together for several years, the bond between them can seem unbreakable. But during the 1995 Tournament Players Championship, caddie Mike Mazzeo found that his twenty-year relationship with Fuzzy Zoeller was on shaky ground. Mike had kept Fuzzy waiting on the first tee, claiming he was on a work slowdown because he hadn't been making much money of late. "You're making less now," said Zoeller as he fired him.

In his pre-tournament analysis of the 1986 Masters, *The Atlanta Journal-Constitution*'s Tom McCollister wrote off Jack Nicklaus as "too old, washed up, done." After Jack shot a final-round 65 to win the green jacket, McCollister walked into the crowded interview room and heard Nicklaus say, "Thanks for the inspiration, Tom." "Glad I could help," said McCollister.

Texas has produced almost as many great golfers as it has football stars. Ben Hogan, Byron Nelson, Jimmy Demaret, Tom Kite, and Davis Love III, to name a few. And Texans seem to expect a few fringe benefits wherever they go. In the 1948 U.S. Open at Riviera in Los Angeles, Jimmy Demaret hit to a green but the ball kicked left. As it rolled off the green, the gallery parted and the ball continued into the rough. "Damn," said Demaret, "aren't there any Texans in this crowd?"

TV analyst and former tour pro David Feherty has two favorite sources for his bizarre brand of humor: his experience on the links and his Irish upbringing. An example of the former is his tale of the haughty Senior Tour player whose biggest fear is being in a plane crash and having his body found in coach class. An example of the latter is his story of his father stumbling home after one drop too many at the pub. "Is my dinner still warm?" he asked his long-suffering wife. "Yes," she said, "it's in the dog."

In the early sixties, golf began drawing a respectable TV audience, and televising the big-money match between Byron Nelson and Gene Littler became quite an event. With a TV camera poised about 250 yards down the first fairway, Nelson blasted a huge drive right down the middle. As Littler prepared to hit, a cameraman picked up Nelson's ball and ran it back to the tee. "Would you please hit it again, Mr. Nelson?" he asked. "We weren't ready."

Singer/comedian Phil Harris held the Hollywood Drinking Championship title for quite a few years. (And that's a pretty tough league.) Once, he and Bing Crosby were golfing in Scotland, and as they drove by a Scotch distillery one evening, Crosby said, "See Phil, they're making it faster than you can drink it." "Maybe," said Harris, "but I've got 'em working nights."

Tommy Bolt was playing a round with a caddie who was getting on his nerves. Finally, after a particularly heated exchange about club selection, Bolt asked a tournament official for a ruling: "I know I can be fined for throwing a club," Bolt said, "but is there a penalty for throwing a caddie?"

England's Lord Robertson loved the game of golf but was more frustrated with it than most. It got to the point where he could think of no shot in which he had confidence. When pressed, however, he admitted to having two favorites: the practice swing and the conceded putt. "The rest can never be mastered," he said.

The Senior Tour has been a boon to many of the older players, including the Senior Señor himself, Chi Chi Rodriguez. Chi Chi also made pretty decent money on the regular tour, but it took him a while. He remembers being congratulated back then on passing the million-dollar mark in earnings. "That's swell," he said at the time, "but I've already passed the two-million-dollar mark in spending."

Ben Hogan was always grateful for the patronage of the pros who used his clubs, and he took their support personally. Gary Player, who had known Hogan for years, was playing erratically in the 1973 Brazilian Open. Between rounds, Player called Hogan for some advice. Ben said, "Gary, what clubs do you use?" "Dunlop," said Player. "Then ask Mr. Dunlop," said Hogan as he hung up the phone.

In the late eighties, as the Senior Tour was gaining popularity, the dapper Doug Sanders admitted modestly to a reporter that there were two players people invariably asked about after every tournament: himself and Arnold Palmer. "They want to know what Arnold shot and what I was wearing," explained Sanders.

Bob Hope has made a specialty out of Gerald Ford golf jokes. But the ex-president gets in a few jabs of his own now and then. Asked about Hope's goal of shooting his age, Ford said, "I know he'll do it someday, even if he has to live to be 125."

No hole-in-one hysterics for songwriter and avid golfer Hoagy Carmichael. Teeing off on a par-3 one day, he hit a shot that took one bounce on the green, hit the pin, and dropped directly into the hole. Without skipping a beat, he pulled out another ball, teed it up, and said, "I think I've got the hang of this now."

Bill Davis was one of the founders of *Golf Digest* and ran the magazine for many years. He was smart but quirky and unpredictable, and some of his eccentricities drove many of his writers to distraction. At his retirement dinner, he spoke of the editor's relationship with the writer. "Even Hemingway would have been a better writer if I had edited him," he bragged. "True," agreed a writer in the audience, "but he'd also have committed suicide ten years sooner."

If a record exists for the fewest words spoken during a golf match, tight-lipped Harry Vardon probably holds it with one. In a tense match with Bobby Jones, Vardon had said nothing through 17 holes. Then, on 18, Jones skulled a fairway shot and, furious with himself, screamed, "DID YOU EVER SEE SUCH A TERRIBLE SHOT!" "No," said Vardon.

Lee Trevino is not particularly fond of British courses. After a practice round before a British Open at St. Andrews, Trevino complained about the thick rough he and his caddie plunged into near the 15th green. Someone asked if they found the ball. "Yes, we found the ball," said Trevino, "but we lost the bag."

Tony Kornheiser of the *Washington Post* shares a goal with many amateur golfers: breaking 100 consistently. However, as he looks ahead, Tony sees little chance of reaching the goal of many senior players: shooting one's age. "I'll be lucky to shoot my body temperature," he says.

Thanks to the Senior Tour, Chi Chi Rodriguez is making more money than ever, and his theatrics on the course are getting as many laughs as they ever did. One difference he's noticed, however, is his distance off the tee. "The older you get," he says, "the longer you used to be."

Byron Nelson is one of the greatest golfers of all time, but he's also a realist. Greg Norman won the Byron Nelson Award in 1995, and as Nelson was handing him the trophy, Norman said, "Byron, I'm just sorry that you and I never had a chance to compete against one another." "I'm not," said Nelson.

At the 1993 Houston Open, a longest-drive contest was held between John Daly and Jim Dent. The deal was that you could take two swings, but if you chose to hit the second ball, that's the one that counted. Dent hit his first ball 318 yards and settled for that. Daly's first shot went 321 yards, but he said, "No, I didn't hit that one very well. I'll try another." The mulligan went 340 yards.

There's something about golf that seems to attract politicians, especially presidents and governors. Former California governor George Dukmejian knew enough about golf and government to explain how the two differ: "In golf, you can't improve your lie."

Lee Trevino is like most golfers in at least one respect: He has trouble hitting the 1-iron. So why does he carry the club? Apparently for holding straight up in the air while walking off a course as lightning threatens. "Not even God can hit a 1-iron," he explains.

If you're looking for the odds that an amateur will shoot a hole-in-one, Lloyds of London will quote you 12,600 to 1. And that includes the ones that bounce off a tree or rock or someone's head. Contrast this information with a bit of insight from writer Martha Beckman: "People blame fate for other accidents, but feel personally responsible for a hole-in-one." (from *Meditations to Make You Smile*)

You never know which Billy Casper is going to show up at the next senior tournament: the 220-pound Billy Casper (at one U.S. Open) or the 180-pound Billy Casper (at the next one). His buffalo meat diet, among others, has kept his tailors busy and happy. As ex-quarterback John Brody put it, "Billy Casper has won more titles at more different weights than Sugar Ray Leonard."

One of the few black days in the golfing life of
Jack Nicklaus was the opening round of the
1987 British Open. Nothing went right that day, and
Jack carded a miserable 83. Not everyone was
unhappy though. Broadcaster Paul Harvey was overheard in the gallery saying, "All my life I've wanted to
play like Jack Nicklaus...and now I can!"

When it comes to married-couple competition,
few can compete with Judy and Gardner
Dickinson. There was a time, however, when Judy was
riding high on the LPGA Tour and Gardner wasn't
doing too well in PGA play. Apparently, their relationship wasn't doing too well either. During one of their
domestic spats, Judy took a very cheap shot: "Oh God,
Gardner," she said, "sometimes I think you married me
just to see your name on the leader board."

Walter Hagen was quick to recover from a mistake. Once, in England, while ad-libbing the acceptance speech for the victorious American Ryder Cup team, he said, "I am indeed proud to captain the first American Ryder Cup to win on home soil." When several in the audience yelled out, "Foreign soil, Walter," he smiled and said, "Now, you can't blame me for feeling completely at home here, can you?" The audience loved it.

TV commentator Gary McCord eventually took Ben Hogan's advice. Gary had been struggling on the regular pro tour for quite a while when he was introduced to Hogan. Not recognizing McCord, Hogan asked him what business he was in. "I'm a professional golfer," said McCord. "How long have you been on the tour?" asked Hogan. "Ten years," said McCord. "And how many tournaments have you won?" "None," said McCord. "Don't you think it's time you found a real job?" asked Hogan.

In recent years, the American team has taken the Ryder Cup competition very seriously, while the Europeans have continued to think of it as a bit of good fun. That is, until the 1999 matches, if European captain Mark James's remarks are to be taken at face value. As the competition started, James said, "We're both out here to win the matches. But at the end of the week, [U.S. captain] Ben Crenshaw and I will be able to sit down and have a beer, and I'll be able to shake him warmly by the throat."

Robert Trent Jones was taking a lot of heat for his 1954 U. S. Open re-design of the par-3 fourth hole at Baltusrol. So he and a few committee members walked out to the tee box at 4, where Jones dropped a ball and hit it...right into the cup. He turned to the group and said, "The hole certainly seems fair to me."

Chi Chi Rodriguez is best known for his humorous antics on the golf course, and he often combines fun with a bit of hustling. Once, while playing a not-so-friendly nassau at a course in Puerto Rico, he closed out his opponent on the 17th hole and then offered him an attractive press on 18. "I'll give you two strokes and you give me one throw for all the marbles," said Rodriguez. They agreed, and both reached the par-4 green in two, with Rodriguez away. "I think I'll take my throw now," said Rodriguez. And with that he picked up his opponent's ball and tossed it far out into the ocean. "With your drop, you're now lying four," said Rodriguez. "*And* you're away."

Sometimes, telling the truth can get a guy in trouble. Sam Snead was standing on the 16th fairway at Firestone consulting his caddie about his shot. "Jay Hebert hit an 8-iron from here yesterday," the caddie said. So Sam pulled out his 8-iron and hit the ball right into the lake guarding the green. "Where did Hebert hit his 8-iron yesterday?" asked Snead. "Into the lake," said the caddie.

Does Brent Geiberger ever get tired of hearing about his father, Al, becoming the first pro to shoot a 59 in a PGA event? Well, when Brent won the 1999 Greater Hartford Open, he at least put a new spin on the matter. "I shoot 59 every time I play," he said. "Of course, at that point I usually have a few holes left."

In 1992, members of the Boston Amateur Golf Society launched an earnest campaign to increase membership in their Women's Section. When they did not meet with much success, someone pointed out that it might have something to do with their logo and the Society's acronym: BAGS.

Lee Trevino and Chi Chi Rodriguez were in Minnesota just before the 1970 U.S. Open at Hazeltine, and they decided to rent a boat and do a little fishing on one of the state's ten thousand lakes. They found a great spot and hauled in a huge catch of largemouth bass. As the sun started to set and they prepared to head back in, Rodriguez suggested that Trevino mark the lucky spot in case they had a chance to come back. Upon reaching the dock, Rodriguez asked Trevino how he had marked the place. "Right here on the side of the boat," said Trevino. "That's no good!" said Rodriguez. "What if we don't get the same boat?"

When South African golfer Fulton Allem first came to the United States to try his luck on the pro tour, he was beset with various kinds of culture shock, not the least of which was the increasing aversion to smoking in this country. "I was familiar with the old slogan, 'I'd walk a mile for a Camel,'" Allem said, "but now it seems you have to walk a mile to smoke one."

At St. Andrews once, an American had been assigned an old, gnarled caddie who had already carried a full round. The American wondered whether the elderly gnome was up to the task a second time. Nevertheless, they started out, and the Yank played miserably, making the turn in a shaky 55. They were about three holes into the back nine when the caddie picked the man's errant drive out of the gorse, put it in the bag, and turned back to the clubhouse. "I'm sorry," the American said, "I didn't think you'd make it around." "Oh, I'm fine, sir," said the caddie, "but you've had enough for one day."

At the 1975 British Open at Carnoustie, Jack Nicklaus and Tom Watson were shooting an evening practice round when they got a taste of flinty Scottish reserve. On a difficult par-3, with the green tucked behind some mounds, they both hit good tee shots but weren't sure how they turned out. Upon reaching the green, they saw Nicklaus's ball and eventually found Watson's...in the hole. Marveling at the lack of excitement from the small gallery, Nicklaus approached two elderly gentlemen and asked if they saw Watson's ball go in. "Aye," said one of the men, "but it's only practice, isn't it?"

Just because Arnold Palmer is probably the best-recognized golfer of all time doesn't mean *everyone* knows him. Palmer once did a TV commercial that required him to hit shots onto a green. As Arnie hit ball after ball at the flag, one of the camera crew was so impressed that he commented to a fellow worker, "This guy is wasting his time being an actor. He could be a pro golfer!"

Old-timer Jackie Burke thinks that with swing coaches and mental coaches and the like, the modern golf game has become too complicated. "Jimmy Demaret and I had the best golf psychiatrist in the world," he says. "His name was Jack Daniels, and he was waiting for us after every round."

In the 1946 PGA Championship at the Portland Golf Club, Ben Hogan thrashed Jimmy Demaret in the finals, ending the match up 10 and 9. A reporter asked the humbled Demaret if there had been a turning point in the match. "Yes," said Jimmy, "when Ben showed up."

A lot of golfers make the game sound much too complicated. Seve Ballesteros believes in keeping it simple. In the 1988 Masters, he had a four-putt disaster on the 16th green. When the press asked him to explain, he cooperated: "I miss the hole, I miss the hole, I miss the hole, I make it."

The golfing careers of Greg Norman and Chi Chi Rodriguez peaked at different times, but Rodriguez has noticed similarities between the two players. For example, both are referred to as sharks. "Norman's known as the White Shark," explains Rodriguez, "and among my associates, I'm known as the Loan Shark."

One of the early celebrity golf fanatics was singer/comedian Phil Harris, who had a long-running and (we think) friendly rivalry with Jack Lemmon. The one-liners flew thick and fast between them. What did Phil think of Jack's game? "Lemmon's been in more bunkers than Eva Braun," he said.

This is, perhaps, a semi-Freudian slip. A North Carolina tourist brochure reads, "Famous mid-South resorts, including Pinehurst and Southern Pines, have more golf curses per mile than anywhere else in the world."

Ben Hogan had something in common with a lot of pro golfers. He disliked many of the courses designed or remodeled by architect Robert Trent Jones. Hogan thought they were too tough and was not reluctant to criticize Jones's work openly. After being congratulated by Trent's wife, Ione, at the end of a tournament on one of Jones's courses, Hogan coolly responded, "If your husband had to play his courses for a living, you'd both be on the breadline."

Jim Ferree found himself in a delicate situation during the 1960 World Series of Golf at the Firestone Country Club. He had overshot the fourth green and his ball came to rest next to a porta-potty. As he prepared to hit his approach, an official advised Ferree to wait because someone seemed to be in the facility. If the occupant emerged during Ferree's backswing, it would be a distraction. As everyone stood and stared at the outhouse, a muffled voice from inside called out, "Go ahead and hit!"

Variations on the word *golf* go back to the beginning of the game itself, but no one can pin down its exact origin or what the word meant. Writer George Peper has a theory: "According to locker-room lore, the name *golf* arose by default," he says. "All the other four-letter words had already been taken."

Although Ben Hogan was a formidable and intimidating figure, Chris Dunphy was one of the few in golf who stood up to him. Dunphy was the president at Seminole, a course Hogan liked to play when preparing for the Masters. In his later years, Hogan had become a bit deliberate in his putting, and during a round they played together, Hogan complained about the Seminole greens being too slow. "If you didn't take so long to putt," replied Dunphy, "the grass wouldn't be so long."

You've heard that art imitates life, but according to comedian Buddy Hackett, so does fashion. "Once, playing in Georgia, I hooked a ball through some woods and into a swamp," he says. "When I went in to look for it, I found an alligator wearing a shirt with a little golfer on it."

Even though no big-bucks prize money is involved, there's something about Ryder Cup competition that produces emotions and tensions even the majors can't rival. Veteran José Maria Olazabal put it nicely when he described approaching the first shot in Ryder Cup competition: "Everything shakes except the shaft of your club," he said, "and that's because it's still in the bag."

In the second round of the 1925 U.S. Open, Bobby Jones was in danger of missing the cut. On the 11th hole, he pushed a shot into the rough to the right of the green. From there he had apparently lobbed onto the green, but then he announced that his ball had moved in the rough as he first addressed it, and he declared a penalty on himself. He was highly praised for his honesty, but he would have none of it. "That's nonsense," said Jones. "You might as well praise me for not robbing a bank!"

Sports announcers come in all shapes, sizes, and styles. For example, Vin Scully was Mr. Smooth when announcing the action, whereas Dizzy Dean mangled the language. But few could match the sheer poetry of golf announcer Bob Murphy. When describing a delicate approach shot by Lee Trevino back in 1989, Murphy observed, "It came in there like a butterfly with sore feet."

After a long, lonely search, singer/comedian Phil Harris finally found the right caddie: one who drank as well (or at least as much) as he did. Their relationship was strained, however, when one day they both showed up at the first tee in terrible shape. Harris, after some difficulty getting his ball teed up, took a wild and tortured swing at it. "Where did it go?" asked Harris. "Where did what go?" the caddie responded.

Former PGA player Bob Brue claimed he knew a guy whose constant cheating became so much a part of his game that when got a lucky hole-in-one, he put a zero on the card.

You've heard the advice, "Don't get mad, get even!" Well, it took a while, but Arnold Palmer got even. He grew up on the Latrobe Country Club golf course near Pittsburgh, where his father, Deacon, was the club pro. But being an employee's child, Arnie was denied certain member privileges like playing in club tournaments and swimming in the pool. What did he do about it? Years later, after he became rich and famous, Palmer came home and bought the club.

Anyone who remembers the atrocious shirts worn by the 1999 American Ryder Cup team during their fantastic Sunday comeback will appreciate Bud Geracie's theory on what inspired that thrilling performance. Geracie, a writer for the *San Jose Mercury News,* figures it must have been captain Ben Crenshaw's dynamic locker-room speech to the sartorially challenged Americans. He thinks Ben must have said, "Boys, if you're going to wear shirts *that* ugly, you'd better win."

Many are the horror stories that have grown up around the infamous 1-iron. Sportswriter Jim Murray was definitely not a fan of the club. "The only time I ever used a 1-iron successfully was to kill a tarantula," said Murray, "and even then it took me seven strokes to do it."

Show biz celebrities love to play in the Pro-Ams where they can hang around the big hitters on the tour. But what about the pros? Do they like to rub elbows with the stars of stage and screen? Jimmy Demaret didn't seem too impressed a few years back: "Two of my favorite celebrities are comedian Bing Crosby and singer Bob Hope. Or is it the other way around? I always forget which one thinks he's funny and which one thinks he can sing."

What are you going to do when you retire? Most people of the male persuasion respond, "Fish and golf." But among those who find fault with both the question and the answer is long-time pro Julius Boros. When asked late in his career if that were his plan, Julius said, "Why would I want to retire at all? All I do now is fish and golf."

Sounds like Lee Trevino's bank account is so fat he's turning down opportunities to make a few bucks on the side. Lee was washing the front windows of his home in Dallas one day when a car pulled into his driveway. A woman got out and asked him what he charged for that service. "It depends," he said. "At this house, the lady lets me sleep with her."

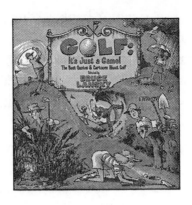

Golf: It's Just a Game!

Selected by Bruce Lansky

This book contains the funniest comments ever made about golf by Lee Trevino, Arnold Palmer, Harvey Penick, Bob Hope, Buddy Hackett, Lewis Grizzard, Gerald Ford, and others. You'll also find clever cartoons by David Harbaugh, Bob Zahn, Lo Linkert, Joe Kohl, and others. Makes a great gift for every golfer.

Order #4035

How To Line Up Your Fourth Putt

by Bobby Rusher

This humorous guide to the game of golf will appeal to any duffer who knows the difference between a wood and an iron. Rusher provides valuable insights you'll never learn from a golf pro, including how to achieve a flawless swing without injuring yourself or loved ones, how to practice proper etiquette when you're playing with a complete jerk, and how to know when to blame the caddie.

Order #4075

Are You Over the Hill?

by Bill Dodds

Everyone knows "old codgers" of 39 or more, and this book is the perfect gag gift to demonstrate just how far they're sliding into decay and decline. It's jam-packed with fun ways to remind friends that their better years may be behind them.

Order #4265

What's So Funny about Getting Old?

by Jane Thomas Noland
Illustrated by Ed Fischer

Do you know somebody who needs some good-natured ribbing about their "advancing age"? Here's a gag gift that will liven up the birthday party of anyone too old to be a member of Generation X. If you know someone whose "head makes promises their body can't possibly keep," you must buy them this book.

Order #4205

What You Don't Know about Turning 50 . . .

by P.D. Witte

This funny birthday quiz contains outrageous answers to 101 commonly asked questions about turning 50. Illustrated with cartoons, this book contains everything you always wanted to know about the big five-o.

Q: How can you increase the heart rate of your 50-year-old husband?

A: Tell him you're pregnant.

Order #4217

What You Don't Know about Retirement . . .

by Bill Dodds

Makes a great retirement gift and provides a funny quiz to make the retirement party fun. When everyone at the office signs the inside cover, it becomes a precious keepsake. Filled with cartoons by Steve Mark.

Q: What's the best way for a retiree to make sure his memoirs are read?

A: Include lots of clues about hidden money.

Order #4216

Also from Meadowbrook Press

✦ *52 Romantic Evenings*
Unlike other romance books that provide only brief outlines of ideas, this book provides everything a couple needs to know to create romantic evenings that will make their relationship come alive. It details complete plans for a year's worth of romance-filled evenings, including where to go, what to wear, what to eat, what to drink, what music to play, and more.

✦ *The Mocktail Bar Guide*
Here is a must-have addition to your collection of bartending and party-planning books. This one-of-a-kind guide offers 200 delicious, alcohol-free drink recipes for nondrinkers, designated drivers, expectant mothers, and anyone who enjoys great-tasting drinks. Royalties from the sale of this book support Mothers Against Drunk Driving (MADD).

✦ *What You Don't Know About Retirement*
"**Q**: How can I make sure my friends and family stay in touch? **A**: Move to a vacation spot and live in a place with a pool. **Q**: Why is it dangerous for a retiree to miss the condo-owners association meeting? **A**: They might be elected president." Makes a great gift and provides a funny quiz to make any retirement party more fun.

We offer many more titles written to delight, inform, and entertain. To order books with a credit card or browse our full selection of titles, visit our web site at:

www.meadowbrookpress.com

or call toll-free to place an order, request a free catalog, or ask a question:

1-800-338-2232

Meadowbrook Press • 5451 Smetana Drive • Minnetonka, MN • 55343